Breathings

Breathings

the Poems of Philippe Jaccottet

translated by Cid Corman

illustrated by Anne-Marie Jaccottet

A Mushinsha Book

Grossman Publishers

First published in the United States of America
in 1974
by GROSSMAN PUBLISHERS
625 Madison Avenue
New York, N.Y. 10022

Designed and produced by Mushinsha Limited
IRM/Rosei Bldg., 4, Higashi Azabu 1-chome, Minato-ku,
Tokyo, Japan
Copyright in Japan, 1974, by Cid Corman
All rights reserved
Printed in Japan
First Edition, 1974
Library of Congress Catalog Card No. 73-89804
SBN: *Hard cover 670-18868-9; Paperback 670-18869-7*

Introduction

Unless to you, to whom should I praise love?| It is a throwaway,
a breath on the air,| gratuitous, as if not elicited.

And how should I feel the absence, the emptiness,| the failure to be
there except as someone not?| It was you, that one, the one not there.

(*William Bronk*:
In Praise of Love)

"...some part of his (the sage's) life considers exclusively the
Soul's satisfaction; the rest is not immediately for the Term's sake
and not for his own sake, but for the thing bound up with him, the
thing which he tends and bears with as the musician cares for his
lyre, as long as it can serve him: when the lyre fails him, he will
change it, or will give up lyre or lyring, as having another craft
now, one that needs no lyre, and then he will let it rest unregarded
at his side while he sings on without an instrument. But it was not
idly that the instrument was given him in the beginning: he has
found it useful until now, many a time."

(*Plotinus,* Enneads, I, *4—MacKenna,*
quoted in La Semaison)

What we are faced with today, more and more, those of us who are attentive and care, are poets who question all word, all act of word, all act. Not that they are vain enough to fall back on mere indolence or self-indulgence. They do make what sense they can through words, while feeling the vacuity of all sense. I think of Beckett and Bronk, du Bouchet and Jaccottet.

Earlier this month I received this letter from Grignan, answering a request for poetry perhaps more recent than his last small collection of "new" poems, *Lessons*. The pertinent sentence goes:

v

"I haven't written any poems since Lessons *((that is, since October 1967)), I don't know at all how that is made, a poem. I still try, sometimes, quite in vain."*

To tell you what you yourself will find in the following pages would be impertinent. The words reveal themselves and in the mode of poetry. That Jaccottet is a poet, a consummate artist, each syllable makes only too articulately clear. His very facility to elicit beauty of language has again and again brought him to self-questioning.

(Sept. 1965) *"What makes expression hard for me now is that I don't want to cheat—and it seems to me that most cheat, more or less, with their own experience; put it between parentheses, make it vanish." ". . . more and more* (March 1966) *I hear the lie of words, which paralyzes me. I'd like misery to strip them bare. It's only a wish. I'm neither uncouth, nor simple."* (Nov. 1959) *". . . questioning is the essence of our nature."*

Beyond the gentle thoughtful ruminated music of his verse, whose often intricate rhyming is beyond the power of translation, there is a ringing quietness, a compelling absence, at work.

(Nov. 1959) *"If I breathe, it's just that I know nothing else." "To speak with this emptiness at heart, against it." "All poetry is the voice given to death."* Even as all the elegiac poems of *Lessons,* celebrating the death of his father-in-law beyond lament, where the words move off like smoke into the larger sky and the dust of words settles like ash upon the old tilled ground, reveal the constant note of mortality, the "invisible bird," so often evoked, is sensed out there within.

(May 1954) *"Self-attachment augments the opacity of life. A moment of true oblivion, and all the screens one behind the other become transparent, in such a way that one sees clear to the end, as far as the view carries; and at the same stroke nothing more weighs. So the soul is truly made into a bird."*

His earlier poems move from place to place, often in the city, but most of those I have drawn on here, following his own emphasis in his recent selected *Poésie* (1946–1967), are decisively situated in Grignan in the Drôme just north of Provence. The nature of the place and of this absent man within it, who hallows it and is hallowed by it, the poems again and again elicit and project. It is intimate and open, a soft cry at moments of given days.

"No castles: streets, rooms, paths, our life."

vi

Jaccottet moves between a feeling for the leverage of precise limits and at the same time a yearning, nostalgia, for the illimitably open

"That of feather that marks a flight—or a nest."

*"Silence, repose, waiting.
One shall have been, once at least, in this place."*

"Out of nothing. That is my law. All the rest: distant smoke."

"Sonority at once sweet and crystalline. But most of all, porous *to the celestial infinite.
Alveoli. A network of words which contain the sky or filter it as do the trees?"*

I call the poems "breathings," but Jaccottet himself has written me, in explaining the word *"semaison"* (which is the title of his most recent work, his notebook selections, from which the quotations I have cited come)—the natural yearly dispersion of seed, that this is the sense he has, hopefully, of his own work.

"It's the All-other that one tries to grasp. How explain that one seeks it and doesn't find it, but that one nevertheless keeps seeking? The unlimited is the breath *that animates us. The obscure is a breath; God is a breath. One cannot get hold of it. Poetry is the word that this breath feeds and bears, from whence its power over us."*

17 November 1972   Utano

The Screech-Owl

1946–1950

Night is a vast city fast asleep
with wind blowing . . . that has come from far to
this bed's asylum. It's midnight in June.
You sleep, I'm drawn out upon these infinite shores,
wind shaking the nut tree. The call comes
approaches and recedes, you would swear
a gleam escaping through woods, or even
shades wheeling about, as fabled, in hells.
(This call of a summer night, how many things
I could say of it, and of your eyes. . . .) But it's
only a screech-owl calling us from deep
within these suburban woods. Already our odor
is that of something decaying at daybreak,
already under our hot skins the bone stabs,
while the stars sink at the corners of streets.

AGRIGENTUM,
January 1st

A little higher than this place with its rare targets,
we look for the staircase from which the sea is visible,
or at least would be if the weather were clear.
—We have travelled for the mildness of the air,
for forgetfulness of death, for the Golden Fleece. . . .
Despite the path taken, we rest at the edge,
and it isn't these hasty words that were our need,
nor this forgetfulness, itself forgotten so soon. . .—
It begins to rain. A year has changed.
You can see that our soul is condemned to regrets:
we must, even in Sicily, accept upon our hands
the thousand thorns of the rain . . .until tomorrow.

TIME WHEN THE WIND
SCATTERS THE SEED

I

We would guard purity,
should evil have more reality.

We would not bear hate,
though the storm stun the seeds.

Who knows how slight the seeds are
would be fearful of adoring thunder.

II

I am the indecisive line of trees
where pigeons in the air beat their wings:
you who are caressed where hair is born. . . .

But under the fingers deceived by distance,
the gentle sun snaps like straw.

III

The earth here is threadbare. But let it rain
just one day, you divine in its humidity
a trouble from which you know it will return anew.
Death, for an instant, has that air of freshness
of the blossoming snowdrop. . . .

IV

Day stands hunched in me like a toro:
one would readily believe it's strong. . .

If one could weary the torero
and a little delay the death blow!

V

In winter, the tree mulls within.

Then laughter one day is abuzz
and the murmur of the leaves,
ornament of our gardens.

For one who loves no one now,
life is always further off.

VI

O first days of spring
playing in the schoolyard
between two classes of wind!

VII

I get impatient and I am worried:
who knows the plagues and who the treasures
another life bears? A springtime can
leap forth in joy or blow towards death.
—Here's the blackbird. A timid girl
goes from her house. Dawn is in the wet grass.

VIII

Far in the distance
I see the street with its trees, its houses,
and the fresh gale of the season
which often changes direction.
A cart goes by with white furniture
into the shadowy underbrush.
The days go on ahead,
what remains me I can swiftly enumerate.

IX

Thousands of insects of the rain have worked
all night long; the trees have blossomed with drops,
the downpour makes the sound of a distant whip.
The sky for all that has remained clear; in the gardens
the tools ringing sound matins.

X

This invisible air
bears a distant bird
and the weightless seeds
from which tomorrow will sprout
the edge of the woods.

Oh! the course of life
stubborn going down!

XI

(The Seine March 14th 1947)

The crackled river turns turbid. The waters mount
and wash the embankment stones. For the wind
like a dark hulking vessel has come down
from the Ocean, charged with a freight of yellow seeds.
There floats an odor of water, far and faint. . . . One trembles,
only from having surprised some eyelids opening.

(There was a canal mirroring what one followed,
the factory canal, one would cast a flower
at the source, to find it again in the city. . . .)
Memory of childhood. Waters never the same,
nor days: he who would gather water in his hands. . . .

Someone lights a fire of branches on the bank.

XII

All this green does not accumulate, but trembles and shines,
like the streaming curtain of fountains one sees
responsive to the least stir of air; and up on top
of the tree, it seems that a swarm has settled
of buzzing bees; easy countryside
where always invisible birds call to us,
voices, uprooted like seeds, and you,
with your curls tumbling over clear eyes.

XIII

Of that Sunday just one moment rejoined us,
when the winds with our fever have fallen:
and under the street lamp, the cockchafers
light up, then go out. One would say—lanterns
far off in a park, perhaps for your birthday. . . .
I too had believed in you, and your light
made me burn, then left me. Their dry husk
falls and is crushed in the dust. Others arise,
others blaze, and I am left in the shade.

XIV

All was a sign to me: the lilacs eager to live
and the children losing their balls in
the parks. Then, patches turned over nearby,
while stripping root after root, the smell
of a hardworked woman. . . . The air wove of these nothings
a trembling web. And I ripped it apart,
by dint of being alone and looking for traces.

XV

The lilacs once more have opened
(but this is no assurance for any now),
redstarts flash, and the voice of the maid
when she speaks to the dogs grows soft. Bees
work in the pear tree. And there is always,
way off in air, that vibration of machines. . . .

THE STREAMS AND THE FORESTS

I

The clearness of these woods in March is unreal,
all is still so fresh that it hardly insists.
Birds are not numerous; all just so,
afar, where the hawthorn lights up the coppice,
the cuckoo sings. Sparks are seen from smoke
bearing away what has been burnt of a day,
the dead leaf serves the living crowns,
and following the lesson of the worst paths,
under brambles, the anemone's nest is rejoined,
clear and common as the morning star.

II

Even if I knew the net of my nerves
as precarious as the spider's web,
I would not praise any less these green wonders,
these columns, though chosen for the axe,

and these woodcutters' horses. . . . My confidence
must be extended one day to the hatchet, the lightning,
if the beauty of March is only the obedience
of blackbird and violet, in clear weather.

III

Sunday peoples the woods with whining children,
ageing women; one boy out of every two bleeds
at the knee, and one returns with soiled handkerchiefs,
leaving old papers by the pool. . . . Cries
recede with the light. Under the yoke-elms,
a girl pulls on her skirt at each alarm,
harassed air. All mildness, that of the air
or of love, has cruelty when turned over,
every fine Sunday has its ransom, as parties
those stains upon the tables when the day disturbs us.

IV

All other anxiety is futile yet,
I shant walk long in these forests,
and the word is neither more nor less useful
than these catkins of willow in the marshes:

no matter that they fall in dust if they shine,
many others will walk in these woods who will die,
no matter that beauty falls and grows rotten,
since it seems in total submission.

The Ignorant

1952–1956

for A.–M.

PRAYER BETWEEN NIGHT AND DAY

At the vague hour when so many ghosts
press up against the panes, drawn there
by a hesitancy between darkness and day
and menacing with their murmurs clarity,

a man prays: beside him stretched out is
the disarmed naked warrior beauty;
and not far off the heir of their battles rests,
keeping Time clenched in his hand like straw.

"A prayer spoken out of fear, difficult
to be answered, and without help from outside;
a prayer amidst the commotion of cities,
with the war's ending, in the afflux of the dead:

that dawn, with her tenacious tenderness,
that the coming of the light along the summits,
as she removes the pale moon, may efface
my own fable, and with her fire veil my name."

NEW NOTES FOR THE TIME
WHEN THE WIND SOWS THE SEED

Now the earth is revealed
and the sunlight turning like a beacon
makes the trees pink and black.
Then writes upon the grass with dilute ink.

*

One evening the sky stayed longer clear
on the great gardens green and black
from the rains of the night before.
The globes glittered too soon.
Then in the nest of branches
appeared the blackbird's song
and it was as if the oil of the light
burned gently in that feeble black lamp,
or the voice itself of the moon
come to predict night in March to those passing. . . .

NOTES FOR DAY BREAK

Women cry in the dust. For to sing,
how would one under these brittle rocks?
The city with its sounds, its caves, its brilliance,
is only one name for these great empires of sand
whose last venture is in shadow and light.
But always, over these gulfs of water, shines the ephemeral. . . .

And this is what I should now like to
be able to say, as if, despite appearances,
it mattered to me that it were said, neglecting
all beauty and all glory: who advances
in the dust has only his breath for all his good,
for all his strength only an uncertain tongue.

*

Webs, woods, wet rocks,
country pursued by water,
like a woman at night,
a warm and rainy beauty.

*

Forest by the sea at dawn,
bristled and steeped by wind,
I enter and choke within you.

*

Indolent as oil,
but oil becomes light,
burns, murmurs, rejoices
in the sweating vigil.

*

Where will you be when death occurs,
moon as lovely as a sun
turned to the seaside wood,
birds risen together,
beautiful workers of dawn?
And you, where will you be when they scarcely awoke,
comparable to nothing in this world
if not precisely to this increasing light,
where will you be, day break?

Not only then, but already now
you are no more than this too feeble voice,
than these words always vague.
O glittering love!
It is soon no more than the call
that those divided release.
(So all reality
in the heart where death is occupied
becomes cry, murmur or tear.)

*

Skylark, star amidst the day,
before it be too late,
before I have done
with these very clear things,
could you bring me again
to the sill of such a night.

THE VOICE

Who sings there when all voice is still? Who sings
with that pure and hushed voice so fine a song?
Would it be beyond the city, in Robinson, in a
garden covered with snow? Or is it there nearby,
someone who didn't think anyone was listening?
Let us not be impatient to know
for the day is not otherwise preceded
by the invisible bird. But let us only make
silence. A voice rises, and like a wind in March
to the old woods gives strength, it comes to us
tearless, smiling rather in the face of death.
Who was singing there when our lamp went out?
No one knows. But only that heart can hear
that seeks neither possession nor victory.

THE IGNORANT

The older I get the more ignorant I am,
the more I've lived the less I possess and rule.
All that I have is a space gradually
lost in snow or aglow, but uninhabited.
Where is the donor, guide, and guardian?
I stay in my room and for a time am still
(silence enters to tidy up things a little),
and I expect one by one illusions will go:
what remains? What remains for the dying
to really prevent his dying? What force
makes him still speak within his four walls?
How could I, ignorant and unquiet, know?
But I do hear him who speaks, and his word
breaks in with the day, although quite vague:

"Like fire, love builds its illumination
only on the fault and beauty of woods in ashes. . . ."

THE WAKE

One doesn't make noise
in the room of the dead:
one raises the candle
and sees them recede.

I raise my voice a little
at the door's threshold
and I say some words
to light up their way.

But those who have prayed
even under the snow,
the bird at break of day
comes to carry their voices on.

THE GYPSIES

for Gérard and Madeleine Palézieux

There's a fire under the trees:
you can hear it whispering
to the nation fast asleep
near the gates of the city.

If we walk in silence,
souls of a little time
between the dark abodes,
it's of fear that you may die,
perpetual murmur
of the light concealed.

REASON

I bestow favors with my hand,
write words wantonly on air,
but at bottom the bottom perhaps is reached.
From dead foot to living eye is close,
you will grasp the distances tomorrow.

THE BOOK OF THE DEAD

I

He who has entered into age's properties,
no longer looks for pavilions or gardens,
or books, or canals, or foliage,
or the trace, in mirrors, of a swifter softer hand:
the eye of man, at this point in his life, is veiled,
his arm too weak to take hold, to overcome,
I look at him looking at all recede
that was once his only task, his dear desire. . . .

Hidden power, if there is one, I beg you,
let him not bury himself in fear of his faults,
let him not harp on love's factitious words,
let his worn potency one last time leap up,
gather itself, and another ecstasy invade him!

His hardest struggles were the flashings of birds,
his gravest hazards merely an invasion of rain;
his loves have never broken anything but reeds,
his glory to write on the wall soon ruined a name of soot. . . .

*

Let him enter now clad only in impatience
into this space at last to his heart's content;
let him enter, with his sole adoration for all science,
into the riddle was the dark source of his tears.

No promise has been given him;
no assurance will be left him now;
no response can reach him now;
no lamp, in the hand of a woman once known,
to light his bed or the interminable avenue:

let him be willing then to wait and only rejoice,
as the wood learns only in defeat to dazzle.

II

Companion who have not yielded in anxiety,
don't let fear disarm you at this pass:
there must be a way to win out even here.
No more—of course—with cheques or standards,
no more with shining arms or bare hands,
nor even with lamentations and avowals,
nor with words, even the most restrained. . .
Sum up all your being in your weak eyes:

The poplars are still standing in the light
of the late season, they tremble by the stream,
one leaf after the other docilely descends,
opening the menace of the rocks ranged beyond.
Strong incomprehensible light of time,
O tears, tears of happiness upon this earth!

*

Soul subjected to the mysteries of motion,
pass borne away by your last wide look,
pass, passing soul that no night stopped
from passion or ascension or smiling.

Pass: there is space between the fields and woods,
there are fires of those whom no shadow can reduce.
Where the eye is buried and quivers like a lance,
the soul penetrates and finds obscurely its recompense.

Take the path your breathless heart pointed out,
turn with the light, persevere with the waters,
pass with the irresistible passage of birds,
disappear: there is end only in unmoving fear.

III

Offering from the poor be offered the poor dead:

a single trembling reed plucked from the edge
of a swift stream; a single word uttered by it
which was for him breath, tender wood and spark;
a memory of light up above in the air. . . .

And let by these three slight blows be open to him
the space without space where all suffering's effaced,
the unilluminate light of the unimaginable face.

IV

These tourbillions, these fires and these cool showers,
these blissful glances, these wingèd words,
all that seemed to me to fly like an arrow
through partitions successively borne away
to a successively clearer and higher end,

was perhaps a ramshackle house of reeds
now in ruins, in flames, consumed,
whose ashes the poor man will rub his back with
and his skull after the passing of armies. . . .

Only ignorance abides. Not death,
nor laughter. A hesitancy of light
under our tents nurses love. The nurse
approaches in the East: at day break a man goes out.

V

But if what I speak of with these almost weightless words
was really behind the windows, this cold such
that advances thundering in the vale? No, for that
still is an inoffensive image, but if
death was really there as it will once have to be,
where will the images be, the subtle thoughts, the faith
preserved through the long life? As I see
the light flee in the trembling of every voice,
drown its force in the funk of the body at bay
and its glory at once too large for the narrow skull!

36

What work, what adoration and what combat
would prevail over this aggression from below?
What look prompt enough to pass beyond,
what spirit light enough, say, will fly off
when the eye fails, when all companions go,
when the spectre of the dust arrests us?

VI

Where this beautiful body descends into the unknown earth,
combatant clad in leather or naked dead belovèd,
I shall paint only a tree that retains in its foliage
the gilded murmur of a passing light. . . .

No one can separate fire from ash, laughter from dust,
no one would have recognized beauty without her dying bed,
peace reigns only over the boneyard and the rocks,
the poor man whatever he do is always between two guns.

VII

The almond tree in winter: who can say if this wood
will soon be clad with fires in the darkness
or with flowers in the light of another day?
So is man fed by the funereal earth.

Airs

1961–1964

Our life is woven of wind.

Joubert

END OF WINTER

Little, nothing to chase
the fear of losing space
is left the wandering soul

But perhaps, lighter,
uncertain of enduring,
is that soul which sings
with voice most pure
the distances of earth

A seedtime of tears
on the changed face,
the glittering season
of unsettled streams:
distress wrinkling earth

Age looks at the snow
receding upon the mountains

In the grass in winter surviving
these shadows less weighty than it,
timid patient woods
are discreet, faithful,

still imperceptible death

Always in the revolving day
this flight around our bodies
Always in the field of day
these tombs of blue slate

Truth and untruth
are reabsorbed in smoke

World no better sheltered
than beauty too beloved,
passing into you is celebrating
kindled dust

Truth and untruth
glow, perfumed ash

MOON AT SUMMER'S DAWN

In the ever clearer air
glistening still this tear
or feeble flame in glass
when from the sleeping mountains
mounts a gilded haze

Remains so suspended
on the balance of dawn
between the promised ember
and this lost pearl

WINTER MOON

To enter darkness
take this mirror wherein
a glacial blaze goes out:

the center of night attained,
you'll see no more reflected there
than a baptism of sheep

Youth, I consume you
with this wood that was green
in the clearest smoke
that ever air has borne away

Soul easily frightened,
the earth at winter's end's
only a tomb of bees

IN THE NIGHT'S LAST QUARTER

Out of the chamber of the beautiful
rose of ember, of embraces
the fugitive pointed out
Orion, Ursa, Umbel
to the umbra accompanied him

Then again in the light,
through the light even worn out,
across the day towards earth
this flight of turtledoves

There where the earth ends
lifted very near air
(in the light where the invisible
dream of God roams)

between rock and reverie

that snow: ermine escapes

O companion of the dark
hearken to what its ash hears
the better to yield to fire:

the abundant waters descend
to the levels of grass and rock
and the first birds praise
the always longer day
the light always more near

In the enceinte of winter woods
without entering you can take hold
of the unique light due:
it isn't the blazing pyre
nor branchy hanging lamp

It is the day upon the bark
love which itself disseminates
perhaps the divine light
to which the ax gives strength

BIRDS, FLOWERS AND FRUITS

A straw way up in the dawn
this slight breath along the ground:
what is it passes thus from body to body?
A source escaped from the mountains' fold,
a firebrand?

One hears no birds amongst these rocks
only, away off, hammers

Any flower is only night's
feigning to be approached

But where its fragrance lifts
I cannot hope to enter
or why it much troubles me
and makes so slow my vigil
at this closed door

All color, all life
is born where the eyes rest

This world's only the crest
of an invisible fire

I walk
in a garden of fresh embers
under their shelter of leaves

a coal burning upon my lips

What burns tearing apart the air's
flush or by brusque uprooting
or by constant receding

In growing big at night
the mountain on its two slopes
nurses two sources of tears

Right at the end of the night
when this breath has arisen
a candle at first
has flickered out

Before the first birds
who can still keep vigil?
The wind knows, crossing the rivers

This flame, or tear turned up:
an obol for the ferryman

An aigrette pink on the horizon
a trail of fire

and in the assembly of oaks
the hoopoe stifling its name

Avid fires, hidden voices
flights and sighs

The eye:
a source that abounds

But from whence come?
From further than the furthest
from lower than the lowest

I think that I've drained the other world

What is it to see?

A dart more acute than the tongue
the course from one excess to another
from the most profound to the most remote
from the most sombre to the most pure

a bird of prey

Ah! the idyll yet again
reascending the deep meadows
with its simple shepherds

for nothing but a clouded cup
at which the mouth cannot drink
for nothing but fresh grapes
gleaming higher than Venus!

I no longer want to try
to fly at the speed of time

to think even one instant
my awaiting motionless

SWIFTS

At the stormy moment of day
at the haggard moment of life
these sickles alevel the straw

All suddenly cry higher
than hearing can go

In this mild heat of day

there are only faint rumors
(hammers that you would take for
heels walking upon flagstones)
in places remote from air
and the mountain is a millstone

Ah! let it flame at last
with the amber fallen to earth
and the lute wood of the walls!

FRUITS

In the orchards' chambers
there are globes hung
that the course of time colors
lamps that time illumes
and whose light is perfume

One breathes under each branch
the lash whose aroma is haste

                    *

There are some pearls in the grass
of nacre that much pinker
the less remote the mists are

pendants the heavier
the less linen they adorn

                    *

O how long they sleep
under thousands of green eyelids!

And how the heat

with haste revived
makes their eyes avid!

The shadow slowly of the clouds
like an afterdinner nap

Divinities of plumes
(simple image
or bearing under wing as yet
a true reflection)
swans or only clouds
hardly matters

It's you who have counseled me
languorous birds
and now I look upon it
amidst its linen and its scaly keys
under your distracted plumage

Lightning in August

A shock of hair shaken
sweeping powder from cheeks

so emboldened even lace
is a heaviness

Fruits with bluer weather
as if asleep under a mask of dream
in the blazing straw
and dust of late summer

Shimmering night

Moment when you would say
that the source itself takes fire

The concern of the turtledove
is the first step of day

breaking what the night binds

Leaves or flashings of the sea
or time that shines dispersedly

These waters, these fires together in the combe
and the mountains suspended:
my heart suddenly fails me,
as if lifted up too high

Where none can stay or enter
is what I have hurried towards
the night come
like a looter

Then I've picked up again the reed that measures
the tool of the condemned

Images more fleeting
than the passing of the wind
bubbles of Iris where I slept!

Who closes and reopens
rousing this uncertain breath
this sound of paper or silk
and of light wooden strips?

The sound of tools so distant
it could hardly be called a fan?

For a moment death seems vain
desire itself is forgotten
for what folds and unfolds
before the mouth of dawn

FIELD OF OCTOBER

The perfect mildness is figured from afar
at the limit between the mountains and air:

distance, long spark
tearing apart, refining

All one day the humble voices
invisible birds
hour struck in grass on a golden leaf

the sky so much the greater

The goats in the pasture
are a libation of milk

Where the eye of earth is
no one knows
but I know shadows
it appeases

Scattered wide, one sees better the extent
of the future

Earth entirely visible
measurable
full of time

suspended by a plume that rises
more and more luminous

Apples scattered
over appletree floor

Quick!
Let the skin turn crimson
before winter!

In the expanse
nothing more than shimmering mountains

Nothing more than ardent looks
intersecting

Blackbirds and doves

BIRDS

Flames incessantly changing direction
and hardly visible when they pass

Cries in motion in space

Few have vision enough to see
to sing even in the night

DAWN

You'd say a god is waking up,
looks upon greenhouses and wellsprings

His dew upon our murmurs
our sweats

I have trouble renouncing images

The ploughshare must cut through me
mirror of winter, of age

Time must scatter seed in me

TREES I

From world confused, opaque
with skeletons and seeds
they patiently tear free

so as to be each
more sifted by air

TREES II

From ilex to ilex if the eye wanders
it is conducted through trembling mazes
through swarms of sparks and shadows

to a grotto scarcely more profound

Perhaps now that there's no stele any more
there's no longer any absence or oblivion

TREES III

Trees, tenacious laborers
gradually lighting earth

And so the long-suffering heart
perhaps, purifies

I shall keep within my eyesight
as a redness rather of sunset than of dawn
which is appeal not to day but to night
flame which would like to be hidden by the night

I shall have this mark on me
of nostalgia for the night
even should I go through it
with a billhook of milk

There will always be in my eye however
an invisible rose of regret
as when above a lake
the shadow of a bird has passed

And clouds way up in the blue air
icy curls

vapor of the voice
listened to forever slain

WORLD

Weight of rocks, of thoughts

Dreams and mountains
haven't even balance

We dwell as yet in another world
Perhaps the interval

Flowers blue color
mouths fast asleep
sleep from the depths

You periwinkles
thronging
speaking of absence to one passing

Serenity

The shadow which is in the light
so like a blue smoke

Little matters to me the world's beginning

Now its leaves move
now it's an immense tree
whose sorry wood I touch

And the light through it
shines tears

Accepting's impossible
and understanding too
you cannot will to accept or understand

You move on step by step
like a pedlar
from one dawn to another

VIATICUM

Bird out of the forge

In the afternoon dust
in the dunghill reek
in the light of the square

Could you only
have seen it without knowing it
before moving from the village

Wasn't it
indestructible?

World born of a slit
appeared to be smoke!

Nonetheless the lamp lit
over unending book

WISHES

I

I've long desired dawn
but cannot bear the sight of sores

When will I ever grow up?

I've seen mother-of-pearl:
did I have to close my eyes?

If I am lost
lead me now
hours laden with dust

Perhaps in mingling slowly
pain with light
will I advance one step?

(In the unknown school
to learn the path that passes
through the longest and the worst)

II

What then is the song?
Only a sort of regard

If it could still inhabit the house
in the manner of a bird
which would nest even in ashes
and which flies through tears!

If it could at least protect us
until we are confounded
with the blind beasts!

III

Evening come
gathering all things
into the enclosure

To milk, to feed
To clean out the trough
for the stars

To set the near in order
spreads in the expanse
like the sound of a bell
around itself

Lessons

November 1966–October 1967

Let him be in the corner of the room. Let him measure as he has long done the lines I assemble, interrogating, reminding me of his end. Let his straightforwardness keep my hand from erring if it tremble.

Once
I the frightened, the ignorant, hardly alive,
covering my eyes with images,
pretended to guide the dying and dead.

I, the sheltered,
spared, hardly suffering poet,
dared trace paths in the abyss.

Now, lamp blown out,
hand more errant, trembling,
I start again slowly in the air.

Grapes and figs
hatched afar by the mountains
under slow clouds
and coolness
can they still help me?

Comes a moment when the elder lies down
almost powerless. One sees
from day to day
him stagger more.

It's not a matter of moving now
like water through the grass:
this doesn't turn round.

When even the task master
is taken so fast so far away,
I look for what may follow:

not the lantern of fruits,
nor the adventurous bird,
nor the purest of images;

rather linen and water changed,
the hand that watches,
rather the heart enduring.

I would no more than remove
what keeps us from the clear,
leave only space
for the goodness disdained.

I listen to old men
who are allied by day,
I learn from their feet patience:

they have no worse disciple.

If not the first blow, it's the first outburst
of pain: that the master, the seed,
be so cast down,
that the good master be so chastised
that he seem a helpless infant
in the bed once again too big—
child without the help of tears,
helpless wherever he turns,
brought to bay, pinned down, emptied.

He hardly weighs any more.

The earth which used to bear us trembles.

What I thought I read in him, when I dared read,
was more than astonishment: a stupor
as before a century of darkness to be hurdled,
a sadness! to see those heaves of suffering.
The unnameable burst the barriers of his life.
An abyss that assails. And for defense
a sadness yawning like an abyss.

He who had always loved his close, his walls,
he who had kept the keys of the house.

Between the furthest star and us
distance, unimaginable, remains yet
as a line, an alliance, as a path.
If there's a place beyond all distance,
it must be there that he was lost:
no further than any star, nor less far,
but already almost in another space,
outside of, drawn beyond measure.
Our metre, from him to us, valueless:
much like a blade broken upon the knee.

Mute. The bond of words begins to come undone
also. He leaves words.
Frontier. For a short time
we see him still
He hears almost nothing.
Shall we hail this stranger when he's forgotten
our tongue? when he no longer stops to listen?
He has business elsewhere.
He has nothing to do now.
Even turned to us,
it's like we only were seeing his back.

Back stooping
to pass under what?

"Who will help me? None can come this far.
Who would hold my hands would not hold those trembling,
who would put a screen before my eyes would not keep me from seeing,
who would be day and night around me like a mantle
could do nothing against this fire, against this cold.
None has buckler against the warrior that beset me,
their torches are already in my streets, all is too late.
Nothing awaits me henceforth but the longest and the worst."

Is this how he grows silent in the narrowing night?

It's over us now
like an overhanging mountain.

In its icy shadow
one is reduced to venerate and to vomit.

Hardly does one dare look.

Some thing's thrust into him destroying him.
What a pity
when the other world thrusts into a body
its wedge!

Don't expect
me to marry light to this iron.

Brow against mountain wall
in the cold day
we are full of horror and pity.

In the day bristling with birds.

One can call it horror, ordure,
pronounce even the words of ordure
deciphered in squalor's linen:
whatever silliness the poet allows himself,
it won't get into his formal writing.

Ordure not to be spoken of nor seen:
to be devoured.

All the while
simple as dirt.

Can it be that the darkest night
doesn't cover it?

The unlimited couples or tears apart.

One smells a must of old gods.

Misery
like a mountain fallen upon us.

To have made such a gaping rent,
it cannot be simply a dissipating dream.

Man, if he were only a knot of air,
would he need, to undo it, so cutting an edge?

Stuffed with tears, all, head against this wall,
rather than its insubstantiality,
isn't it the reality of our life
that we are taught?

Instructed by the lash.

A simple breath, a slight knot of air,
a seed escaped from the wild grass of Time,
nothing but a voice that would fly and sing
athwart the shadow and the light,

are they effaced, without the trace of a wound.
The voice kills, one would say rather for an instant
the appeased expanse, the purer day.
What are we, to need this blade in the blood?

One rips it, one roots it out,
this room in which we are locked is rended,
our fibre cries out.

If it were the "veil of Time" which were torn,
the "cage of the body" which were broken,
if it were the "other birth"?

One would pass through the eye of the scar,
one would enter alive the eternal. . . .

Midwives so calm, so strict,
have you heard the cry
of a new life?

I have seen only wax lose its flame
and not the place between these dry lips
for the flight of any bird.

No more breath.

As when the morning wind
has had satisfaction
of the last candle.

There is in us so deep a silence
that a comet
enroute to the night of the daughters of our daughters
would be heard.

Already it's no more him.
Breath ripped out: unrecognizable.

Cadaver. A meteor is less remote to us.

Take it away.

A man (this aerial chance,
frailer under lightning than insect of glass or tulle,
this rock of grumbling kindness and smiles,
this vase the heavier for tasks, for memories),
rip out his breath: so much rot.

Who is avenged, and how, by this spit?

Ah, let this place be swept.

I lifted my eyes again.

Behind the window
amidst the light
images even so pass.

Turnips or angels of being,
they repair space.

The child, in his toys, chooses, as set down
close to the dead man, a boat of earth.
Will the Nile be flowing to that heart?

Long ago I looked at those boats from the tombs
looked like crescent moons.
Today I don't believe the soul can use them,
nor any balm, nor any chart of the Hells.

But if the tender invention of a child
has gone from our world,
has it rejoined him whom nothing rejoins?

Or is it us it consoles on this shore?

If it could be (who will ever be sure?)
that he may still have a kind of being today,
of consciousness even might be believed near,
would it then be here that he would stay
where there's no more than ashes for his hives?
Could it be that he would stay here awaiting
(say) a rendezvous arranged "by the stone,"
that he should need our visits or our tears?
I don't know. One day or another will see
these stones sink into eternal grass,
late or soon there are no more ghosts to invite
to the marker in due time buried too,
nor even shadows in any shade.

Rather, leave taken, I've had but a single desire:
to set my back to this wall
no longer to face away from the light of day,
to better help the waters that originate in these mountains
in shaping the cradle of the grass,
in bearing under the low branches of the figs
through the August night
the boats full of sighs.

And I now utterly in the celestial cascade,
from top to bottom couched in the hair of the air
here, peer of the most luminous leaves,
hung hardly less high than the buzzard,
watching,
listening
(and the butterflies are so many lost flames,
the mountains so much smoke)—
an instant, embracing the whole circle of heaven
around me, I believe death comprised in it.

I see almost nothing other than light,
the cries of distant birds are its knots,

all the mountain of day is lit up,

it no longer hangs over me,

it sets me aflame.

You however,

whether completely effaced,
and leaving us less ashes
than fire an evening at the fireplace,

or invisible inhabiting the invisible,

or seed in the chamber of our hearts,

whatever,

abide as the model of patience and smiling
like the sun on our back as yet
lighting the table, and the page, and the grapes.

PHILIPPE JACCOTTET was born in Moudon (Switzerland) in 1925. After his studies in literature in Lausanne, he lived some years in Paris and worked for the publisher Mermod. Upon marrying, in 1953, he moved to and settled at Grignan, in the Drôme, just north of Provence.

Apart from his own work he has published well-known translations of Hölderlin, Rilke, Musil, and Ungaretti, amongst others.

His four volumes of poetry are represented here, the last two almost in entirety. His prose works are very close to poetry, and often enter into verse: as in *Éléments d'un songe* (Gallimard) or *La semaison* (1954–67) (Gallimard), the latter his most recent work, his notebook journal. His one work of fiction, *L'obscurité* (Gallimard) is an imaginative account of his poetic apprenticeship.

Requiem, Mermod, 1947
L'effraie et autres poésies, Gallimard, 1953
La promenade sous les arbres, Mermod, 1957 (prose)
L'ignorant, Gallimard, 1957
Éléments d'un songe, Gallimard, 1961 (prose)
L'obscurité, Gallimard, 1961 (narrative)
La semaison (Carnets 1954–1962), Payot, 1963
Airs, Gallimard, 1967
Gustave Roud (critical edition), Seghers, 1968
L'entretien des muses (poetry reviews), Gallimard, 1968
Leçons, Payot, 1969
Paysages avec figures absentes, Gallimard, 1970
Rilke par lui-même, Seuil, 1970 (critical study)
Poésie 1946–1967, Gallimard, 1971 (selected poems with an introduction by Jean Starobinski)
La semaison (Carnets 1954–1967), Gallimard, 1971 (augmented edition of the notebooks)